MAP OF INDIA SHOWING BRITISH PROVINCES AND
PROTECTED STATES.

*British Provinces ..   ..   ..   .. Unshaded.*
*Indian States ..   ..   ..   ..   .. Shaded.*

# THE INDIAN STATES
# &
# RULING PRINCES

### By SIR SIDNEY LOW

BooksUlster

First published by Ernest Benn Limited, London, 1929 (Benn's Sixpenny Library, No. 72). This new edition published by Books Ulster in 2016.

Typographical arrangement © Books Ulster

ISBN: 978-1-910375-48-8

Cover illustration is from a painting (*circa* 1793) by Robert Home of Lord Cornwallis receiving the sons of Tipu Sultan as hostage.

# CONTENTS

# FOREWORD

Sidney James Mark Low was born in 1857, the year of the Indian Mutiny. He attended King's College School, London, before going on to Oxford where he studied and graduated in modern history. Venturing into journalism, he was to become the editor of the *St. James's Gazette* and, later, the literary editor of the morning *Standard*. He reported from France and Italy during the First World War and covered, among other major events, the visit of the Prince of Wales (later King Edward VIII) to India in 1921. He was reputed to be balanced in his views and to have a 'pleasant and lively' style of writing. This is certainly evident in *The Indian States and Ruling Princes* which is well-written, clear and thoroughly informative. Low's fair-mindedness is equally apparent and his affection and respect for India is unquestionable. His desire was to see the greatest benefit for the greatest number of its people, although he saw this as best being achieved under some form of British guidance. He believed that independence for the country at that time would prove disastrous ('An independent India is a futile dream') and that dominion status would be rife with inherent problems too. The most likely solution, he felt, would be in some form of federalism, with British-India at the heart of it.

Low acknowledges the impact of the Great War on Anglo-Indian relations and the subsequent growth of Indian self-consciousness in politics:

'New currents were stirring the Indian air in the early years of the present century, and they grew in strength until they gained a fresh and more vivid impulse from the War.'

He nevertheless believed that British influence in India was not set to wane any time soon:

> 'The British bayonet will not fade out of the picture for a long time to come. We are not going to "leave India" to-morrow, or for very many morrows.'

He could not have foretold the advent of the Second World War and the impact it would have on the British Empire and Indian nationalism.

Sidney Low was knighted in 1918. He died in 1932, aged 74, when about to write a weekly article.

Derek Rowlinson
Bangor,
*August*, 2016

# CHAPTER I

## THE TWO INDIAS

INDIA is an empire, but it is not, and never has been, a nation. It is a vast tract of Southern Asia, with diverse races, peoples, and religions, and with many more languages than are spoken in the whole of Europe. So it is, like Europe, a sub-continent rather than a country.

Nor is it a single political unit, though the fact is often ignored in Great Britain and elsewhere. To many, I dare say to most, Englishmen "India" appears as an immense British dependency or subject territory, ruled by an executive responsible to the Parliament and electorate of Great Britain. We suppose vaguely that one government can issue orders, and one legislature make laws, which are valid throughout the whole of the peninsula and its outlying Burmese block. We perhaps imagine that the "Government of India" administers the entire area, in subordination to the "Government" at home.

This is an error. Technically, legally, and politically there is not one India, but two. There is "British India" and there is the India of the Native States. The former is under the direct authority of the Central Indian Executive and Legislature, and indirectly under that of the Cabinet and Parliament. The latter is not a British "possession," but a group of British Protected States, and its inhabitants are not British subjects. It consists of a number of autonomous units, with their own hereditary Princes and Chiefs who are sovereign rulers, except in so far as their sovereignty has been abridged by treaty or agreement with the British Crown. To that Crown they owe loyalty and allegiance, and with it, as representing the British nation and empire, they are in permanent and indissoluble alliance. Their rights and duties are defined by agreements which can only be legally altered by mutual consent.

These States have resigned the conduct of their external and military policy to the Government of India. They have agreed not to communicate directly with foreign Powers. They cannot make war or conclude treaties except with the Paramount Power, or appoint diplomatic and consular agents abroad. They maintain their military forces under conditions as to equipment and armament laid down by the Paramount Power, which has also a certain jurisdiction over European British subjects in certain criminal cases within their borders.

In return for these derogations from their sovereignty they receive protection against violence and aggression. The British Government will defend them against invasion or attack from without, and will intervene when necessary to maintain the lawful authority in the State against rebellion and to check disorder or gross misrule, even to the extent of requiring a ruling Prince to abdicate if he shows himself dangerously incompetent. It watches over the succession to the throne or chiefship, takes care that this passes in a proper and recognised legal manner, and will not allow it to be interrupted by violence or conspiracy. It will not permit the self-government, and administrative independence, of the States to be used to the detriment of contiguous States and Provinces, or to threaten the general tranquillity of the Indian realm.

The Indian Protected territory occupies a larger area, and includes a more numerous population, than is perhaps commonly appreciated. Maps of India are usually tinted in two colours—red to indicate the British Provinces, and yellow or green for the Native States. At a first glance, if the great outlying Burmese polygon be excluded,* it looks as if the yellow or green area were

---

* Burma is by geography, religion, ethnology, and history, altogether distinct from India. Its political association with the Peninsula is very

about as extensive as the red.* It is not; but its size is impressive. It amounts to nearly 40 per cent. of the total extent of India, or about 711,000 square miles out of 1,805,000. The proportionate population is less, because the more densely inhabited Indian districts, such as Lower Bengal, are in the British Provinces. Of the total of 318,000,000, British territory contains 77 per cent. and the Indian States 23 per cent., which amounts to close on 72,000,000, and that happens to be more than the whole white population of the British Empire.

Turn to the map of India again and we notice that the yellow or green colouring is spread over the greater part of the centre of the Peninsula, while the red is mainly along the edges. British territory lies upon the coast and in the fertile, low-lying plains of the great rivers.

The native States rest mostly on the uplands, among the mountains of the northern bastion, or the ridges that stalk through the middle region, and in the elevated tablelands of Rajputana and the Deccan. This distribution points back to Anglo-Indian history in the eighteenth century. Trade, not empire, was what the East India Company wanted. When the pressure of circumstances forced its agents to annex territory they tried to obtain the districts best suited to their mercantile purposes. They preferred the coastal tracts, and the valleys of the great navigable rivers, accessible from the sea, rich in agricultural products, and densely inhabited by a docile population to whom goods from Europe might be sold. "John Company Bahadur" was well content to leave the poorer uplands, with their hunters and intractable, hardy peasantry, to themselves and their own rulers.

The principalities are flung across the main line of

---

recent (Upper Burma and the Siam States were only annexed in 1885), and is not likely to be maintained indefinitely.

* See *Frontispiece*.

communication, and cut off the British Provinces from one another, so that it would be possible to spend a long time in India,
and see a great deal of it, and yet scarcely touch British territory
at all. Indeed, some years ago, a brilliant French writer did that
very thing.* The only India he thought it worth while to describe
was that in which the British do not rule and are seldom seen.
This is the distorted vision of an unfriendly observer, but it may
remind us that one might travel through the length and breadth
of the Peninsula, from the ice-peaks of the Himalayas to Cape
Comorin far down in the tropics, or from the Bay of Bengal on
the East Coast to the Arabian Sea on the West, without spending
more than a few hours at any time on British soil. The Protected
portion would look even larger than it does if we included in it
the broad ribbon of Nepal which stretches for 500 miles along and
below the northern mountain barrier. But Nepal is an independent
allied kingdom, outside the Indian political system, though in
close association with it. The neighbouring small Buddhist State
of Bhutan may also be called independent, since it has neither
the rights nor the obligations of a Protected principality. It has,
however, unlike Nepal, agreed to conduct its external relations
by the advice of the Government of India.

---

* Pierre Loti, *L'inde sans les Anglais* (1903).

# CHAPTER II

## WHAT THE STATES ARE AND WHERE

THIS great Protected territory, which is fourteen times the size of England, is strewn capriciously over India. The actual number of its constituent members is large. There are 448 States, principalities, and lordships, which are not incorporated in the Indian Provinces, and are not under the direct or complete administrative control of the local and central governments.

The great majority of these are very small, and some of them, especially those in the Bombay Presidency, are little more than village groups, over which the chief local territorial proprietor exercises some administrative and fiscal authority, and a limited jurisdiction which does not include the power to inflict capital punishment on criminals. They are land-owners with special hereditary privileges.

There is some excuse for calling these nobles "feudatories," a term which is often, but incorrectly, applied to the whole body of Princes and Chiefs. Feudalism in medieval Europe was based on the tenure of land by homage and military service, due from the holder to his lord, and from that person to his superior. No such system exists in India. To call the Princes the "feudatories" of the suzerain or Paramount Power conveys a wrong impression. But the position of many of the minor Chiefs, particularly in Western India, and in the Chota Nagpur and Orissa districts, does bear some resemblance to that of the barons in England who exercised a certain authority over their dependents, and had their own subordinate courts of justice.

These minute principalities, though numerous, occupy a very small part of the Protected area. Much the larger portion is under the Ruling Princes, who possess full internal sovereignty, except in so far as this has been limited by agreement or understanding. These States are of substantial extent, varying from the dimensions of an English county to those of one of the greater European kingdoms or republics. In India the importance of a potentate or high official is roughly gauged by the number of guns fired in his salute. There are 60 States whose rulers are entitled *ex officio* to salutes of 13 to 21 guns* and another 66 who have 11 guns. It is worth noticing that the 24 States in the first three classes (21, 19, and 17 guns each) comprise much more than half the territory, and two-thirds of the population, of the whole.

There are five first-class (21-gun) principalities—namely, Baroda, Gwalior, Hyderabad, Kashmir, and Mysore; and six of the second class (19-guns)—Bhopal, Indore, Kolat, Kolhapur, Travancore, and Udaipur. All these are extensive and populous countries, and so are several of the third (17-gun) class, which comprises Bikaner, Jaipur, Jodhpur, Patiala, and Rewa. Hyderabad, the Nizam's dominion, is as large as England and Scotland, and has 13 millions of inhabitants. Kashmir is nearly as extensive, though its population is only 3¼ millions. Mysore has a slightly less area, and a slightly larger population, than Ireland. Travancore almost equals Wales in size, with twice as many people. Gwalior has about the same population as Denmark, and a much greater territory.

We may take a brief survey of the principal States without attempting a complete description, or even enumeration. The most

---

* Besides the "permanent" salutes, to which they are entitled as rulers of their States, some of the Princes have been awarded additional salutes, because of their personal distinction or public services. Among those so honoured are the Maharajas of Bikaner, Patiala, Indore, and Travancore, and the Maharana of Udaipur, who each receive two extra guns as "personal" salutes.

northerly is Kashmir (properly Kashmir and Jammu), lying far up beyond the Punjab plain among the valleys of the Hindu Kush, the Karakoram Range, and the Western Himalayas. Some of the highest mountains of the globe are within its borders, and from its flowery glens and blue waters the tourist can look away to the pinnacles of Nanga Parbat and Godwin Austen, and the other snow-clad giants from whose shoulders the Indus, the Chenab, and the Jhelum pour their floods into Hindustan. Kashmir was an outlying wedge of the Moghul Empire, and became first Afghan and then Sikh when that Empire decayed. For five hundred years the country has been one of the great silk producers of the world, and the "Cashmere" fabrics have been worn by multitudes of persons who did not know whence they came. It has much other potential wealth in coal, zinc, copper, gold, and lead, and in due course no doubt will be freely exploited. It is quite prosperous, with a revenue of Rs.2,35,00,000 annually, a land settlement carried out some time ago by Sir Walter Lawrence, and a climate and scenery which poets have praised for centuries and cannot praise too much.

Westward of Kashmir, thrown out among the rugged border hills, there are the small North-Western Frontier States. Then comes a slice of territory, stretching along Afghanistan to Persia, occupied and administered by Britain, so as to keep hold of the railway to our Quetta *place d'armes* and the road to Kandahar. Southward of this pink ribbon lies Baluchistan, divided among several Protected Chiefs, of whom the most important is the Khan of Kalat, with his 54,000 square miles, 300,000 subjects, and a 19-gun salute.

Due south of Kashmir we come to the Protected Punjab States. These include the considerable Mohammedan principality of Bahawalpur, and the Sikh group, of which the most important is Patiala, with a population of 1,500,000, whose able and enegetic Maharaja represented the Ruling Princes of India in the Imperial War Cabinet and at the League of Nations Assembly at Geneva.

It has been allied with the British Government since 1803–1804, and it remained loyal to the alliance through the Sikh War, and the Mutiny, besides several frontier campaigns; and it rendered substantial aid in the Great War. Patiala is irrigated by branches of the Western Jumna Canal system, it has its own railway, and is well cultivated and productive.

Another well-managed and promising State is Kapurthala, chiefly inhabited by Mohammedans, but under a Sikh dynasty, which also has done good service to the British Power. Jind, Nabha and Sirmur are other prominent members of the Punjab group, the whole of which has been in close and friendly relationship with Great Britain since the collapse of the formidable Sikh confederacy after the campaign of 1849, and in the case of some of the States much longer.

South of the Punjab lie the two Protected aggregates known officially as the Rajputana Agency and the Central India Agency. They cover a lot of space on the map, and, in fact, are larger than any of the British Provinces except Burma; but a good deal of this is the western desert tract, large portions of which are scarcely habitable or suited to cultivation. The Rajputana Agency includes the famous States and cities of Rajasthan, the seats of the Rajput clans, whose long and splendid struggle against the Moslem invaders has been told in one of the great prose epics of the English language.

In the early decades of the nineteenth century many of the Rajput States entered into alliance with the English against their common enemies the Mahrattas. Udaipur, with its exquisite capital bathed by a lake of fairyland, counts as the premier of these States, and its dynasty has the longest and most illustrious pedigree of all the Indian reigning families. Jaipur and Jodhpur are larger and more populous; and other historic Rajput centres are Alwar, Jaisalmer, Kotah, Bundi, and Karauli, with one Mohammedan principality, that of Tonk.

Away to the north is the desert State of Bikaner, whose hot winds and sand dunes have not prevented it from being the home of a brisk, busy, and thriving people, fine warriors in the past, and among the keenest traders of India in the present. Under the ruling Maharaja the tradition of valour and statesmanship has been brilliantly maintained. His Highness has led his Camel Corps and Infantry beside the British battalions in China, Egypt, and Palestine, and has seen active service in France. He has attended Cabinet Meetings and Peace Conferences, affixed his signature to the Treaty of Versailles, and was the first Chancellor of the Chamber of Indian Princes.

There is a good deal of modernity about these Rajput States despite their picturesque survivals of Eastern medievalism. Some of them are making notable progress with education, and are encouraging railway developments and irrigation. The rose-red city of Jaipur, which had tried systematic town-planning long before such a thing was thought of in Europe, possesses one of the best Schools of Art and Museums in India, and makes excellent inlaid metal ware. Bikaner is another progressive State, which owns its five hundred miles of railway, and is generally well administered and looked after. I remember some years ago visiting the Maharaja of Bikaner's prison, where I saw the inmates making carpets in apparent comfort and contentment, and I thought the directors of our own penal establishments might have derived some useful hints from it.

To the south of Rajputana lie Baroda and the States of the Central India Agency, joining up with Chota Nagpur and Orissa, and so making a broad band of native-ruled territory stretching right across India. Baroda is one of the five first-class principalities, about the size of Wales, well governed, and progressive. Gwalior, with a population of over three millions, is another of the "Big Five" (21-gun) States. Indore and Bhopal come into the second class. The latter is Mohammedan, and ranks next after Hyderabad among the Moslem-ruled Indian districts.

Baroda, Gwalior, and Indore were carved out of the great Mahratta dominion by the Gaekwar, Scindhia, and Holkar, military leaders who were able to assert their independence of the Peshwa, the nominal head of the confederacy. Their relations with the East India Company till nearly the middle of the nineteenth century were agitated, with constant friction, and a fair amount of fighting. In due course settlements were reached by treaty, and the Mahratta States became friendly and loyal. Their forces and resources have been freely placed at the disposal of the Paramount Power in recent wars.

Coming down to the western coast we reach the peninsula State of Cutch, surrounded by the sea and the great salt lagoons, with about half a million inhabitants. It was known to European traders and travellers earlier than most of India, and has always retained its independent individuality.

The neighbouring peninsula of Kathiawar has been split up among a large number of small principalities and petty chiefdoms. The premier State is Nawanagar, whose ruler, His Highness the Jam Sahib, is better known to the world as Ranjitsinhji, the famous "Ranji" of the English cricket fields.

The great square of the Hyderabad State, the Nizam's territory, occupies the centre of the southern triangle of India. Hyderabad is the first among the principalities in size, population, and political importance. It is 82,000 square miles in area, and the Nizam has actually more subjects than any of the great independent Mohammedan sovereigns—the Shah of Persia, the Amir of Afghanistan, or the Sultan of Morocco.

The Nizam derives from the Viceroys of the Moghul Emperors, sent to rule over the Aryo-Dravidians of the South, who threw off the control of Delhi and made themselves masters of the Deccan. In the latter eighteenth century the Nizam, hard pressed on the one side by the Mahrattas, and on the other by

Hyder Ali, the Mohammedan adventurer who had mastered the Carnatic, entered into alliance with the East India Company. When Hyder Ali's son, Tipu Sultan, was defeated, the Nizam received a share of the territory taken from him. The Hyderabad alliance was tested in the grave crisis of the Mutiny of 1857. "If the Nizam goes, all goes," it was said at the time. But Hyderabad, with a wise sovereign, an able British Resident, and a great Prime Minister, stood fast, and the British raj was saved.

The Nizam's subjects are mainly Tamil and Canarese-speaking Hindu cultivators. But there is a considerable Mohammedan element, particularly in the capital, which in point of population is the fourth city in India, only surpassed by the three great Presidency towns. Many of the "Arabs," as they are called, are descended from the adventurers and soldiers of fortune whom the eighteenth-century Nizams brought in from the outside Moslem world.

Because of its size, political importance, and commanding geographical situation, Hyderabad State has been treated with much respect by the Government of India. We have paid the Nizam the somewhat equivocal compliment of keeping a strong British-Indian force of all arms for his protection (and our security) permanently cantoned in the heart of his dominions. The district of Berar, "assigned" in 1853 by the Nizam in part payment of the expenses of this "Hyderabad Contingent," was leased in perpetuity in 1903, and is now incorporated with the Central Provinces.

Mysore, the second of the Deccan States, is surrounded on all sides by the Madras Presidency districts. It was ruled by Hindu Princes until it passed under the power of Hyder Ali and Tipu Sultan. After the British capture of Seringapatam in 1799 the ancient reigning dynasty was restored; but the country was misgoverned and disorderly, and in 1831 the administration was taken over by the British Government. Fifty years later, in 1881, the

State was reconstituted a protectorate, under special conditions, reaffirmed by treaty in 1913, and the representative of the former dynasty, the father of the present Maharaja, was restored to the *gadi* (throne). Mysore, with its administrative system framed on the best British-Indian pattern, and its long apprenticeship to British rule, is sometimes considered the model Indian State, at least from the political and constitutional standpoint, though the claim might be questioned by some of the others.

The third important State of the Southland is Travancore, stretching between the hills and the sea down to Cape Comorin, the apex of the Indian triangle. It lay outside the range of both Mahratta and Moslem conquest, and has been in alliance with the British since the earlier days of the East India Company, which established one of its factories near Trivandrum in the seventeenth century. Travancore is rather densely populated, with a relatively large number of Indian Christians. It is even more advanced constitutionally than Mysore, having an English barrister as its Dewan or Chief Minister, and an elective Legislative Council.

There are many other interesting States, from Cochin and Pudukotta in Madras to Manipur, high among the mountains of Assam, which cannot be touched upon in this hasty survey. Enough, perhaps, has been said to indicate how varied in character are these principalities, how widely they are distributed, and how significant is their topographical position among and about the Provinces of British India.

All the States have agreed not to enter into direct relations, not only with foreign nations, but with one another. The authority of the Paramount Power in such affairs is exercised through British Residents or Political Agents. In the larger States these officers are appointed by the Central Government, in the minor by the Provincial Governments, and some of the petty chieftainships are under the direction of the local commissioners and district magistrates. The Political Agent at the seat of a Ruling Prince has thus a quasi-diplomatic status. But it is also his duty to report to the Indian Foreign Department on the general condition and internal administration of the unit or group to which he is accredited. On these matters he is entitled to offer his advice to the State rulers, which must be listened to with attention, but is not always, or necessarily, accepted. Of this more will be said later.

# CHAPTER III

## HOW THE STATES ARE GOVERNED

THE Indian Princes, when we entered into alliance with them, were absolute rulers. According to the strict letter of the law they can be so still if they please; for in the treaties and the earlier official declarations their right to govern their dominions in this manner is explicitly recognised. Thus, in the Jaipur Treaty of 1818, it is laid down that "the Maharaja and his heirs and successors shall remain *absolute rulers of their territory and their dependents* according to long established usage." Lord William Bentinck writes to the Nizam telling him that certain promises made to British officers or with their cognisance must be kept; but that "in every other respect *your authority will be absolute.*" The same Governor-General in 1832 said: "I do not possess any authority either to confer or take away the ruling powers in Gwalior, because the Maharaja Scindia *is the absolute ruler of his country.*"

Such blunt statements, which have not been formally repudiated, may seem shocking to some of us in these days of democracy. They did not in the least shock British-Indian negotiators and diplomatists, who knew that autocratic monarchy had prevailed in Asia from time immemorial, and was the only political system that was generally accepted and understood. They saw the less objection to recognising it since they were conscious that the British Crown and the East India Company were themselves autocratic rulers of their Indian subjects and territories.

They knew also that absolute monarchy in an Oriental country does not necessarily mean bad or oppressive government. The

sovereign's autocratic power is exercised under conditions prescribed by religion, usage, and tradition. He is expected to show
regard for law and custom, and to choose for his councillors and
high officials men of learning, wisdom, and character.

Personal monarchy, so regulated and limited, can be efficient
and even liberal. Akbar was an absolute, and Queen Elizabeth, by
comparison at least, a constitutional, ruler. But Hindustan under
the Moghul Emperor was quite as well governed as England under
the Tudors, and Akbar's subjects were not liable to be burnt to
death if their religious views did not precisely agree with those
of their sovereign.

The most effective check on the abuse of autocracy in the East
is public opinion. The monarch, unless he is a military conqueror
with a mercenary army at his back, must not render himself too
unpopular by gross maladministration. If he does so his career is
likely to be stopped short by rioting, revolt, or dynastic conspiracy.

It must be admitted that we weakened the efficacy of these
checks in the native States when we brought them under our protection. At first the Princes gained more than the peoples; for we
guaranteed the throne and the succession against rebellion or any
other movement of violent protest. Under a system of subsidies a
numerous and ill-disciplined body of troops was quartered upon
the larger States, which were subject to many of the abuses of military rule, while the Princes were sheltered against the discontent
it aroused. Our protection, at this stage, was thus a doubtful boon
to the States, since it delayed reforms which otherwise might have
been adopted, and kept them too long backward and disorganised.
The rulers were losing their initiative and sense of responsibility,
and it seemed that other principalities would have to be annexed,
as Oudh was, to save them from complete anarchy.

The subsidiary system was abolished, the unruly prætorians
were withdrawn, and the States put their houses in order. The
recovery was mainly due to the far-sighted energy of a number of

very able Indian statesmen, like Salar Jang of Hyderabad, Madhava Rao of Indore, and Dinkar Rao of Gwalior. Supported by their Princes, and encouraged by British precept and example, these men effected salutary reforms which have taken root and grown. The land settlement, revenue, and police methods of the adjacent Provinces were introduced, and the administration placed under the direction of educated Indians or of English military and civil officers. Several of the Princes are still largely indebted to the advice and assistance of able British ministers and commissioners who have quitted the Anglo-Indian hierarchy to accept important posts in the States.

Thus great improvement in internal government was effected. The progress has not been uniform, and in some of the principalities there is still room for amendment. So recently as in 1926 the Government of India thought it necessary to insist on important administrative changes in the Nizam's dominions. But, speaking generally, life and property are properly protected in the principalities, and public order is as well maintained as in British India, and sometimes better.

The Prince remains the head of the executive; but he now mostly governs with the aid of a durbar and secretariat, or other authoritative advisory body. In most of the larger States there has been instituted some form of ministerial government, and an assembly with more or less ample powers of legislation. Hyderabad has its Executive Council, with a Legislative Council of twenty members, twelve of whom are official. Mysore has its Dewan or Prime Minister, with what may be called a Cabinet, a Legislative Council, and a Representative Assembly, chosen by a rather wide franchise, which is extended to women. This Assembly has the right to be consulted on all measures of legislation, and may discuss finance and taxation. The Legislative Council, with a majority of thirty non-official members, may amend, as well as examine, the State Budget. There are also Standing Committees of both branches of the Legislature on railways, public works, public health, and finance.

No other State has such a full-fledged constitution as Mysore, which had the outline of its political system laid down by the Supreme Government when it was restored to statehood in 1881. Travancore, however, is not far behind, and in some respects even more advanced. It has a Legislative Council with a majority of non-official elected members, which can vote on the Budget, and women exercise the franchise on the same terms as men. There is also a popularly elected Representative Assembly, which has no control over administration, but is entitled to discuss all public affairs and bring its views before the Dewan.

The machinery of consultation and discussion modifies the technical autocracy of the rulers in all the important units. Generally there is a State Council under a Chief Minister, or President, and a Legislative Assembly with a varying proportion of non-official or elected members. Most of the States have also remodelled their judicial and magisterial services in imitation of our own, and have high-court judges, subordinate judicial officers, and district magistrates, with powers and duties resembling those of similar functionaries in British India.

It will be seen that the basis has already been laid for a highly developed constitutional apparatus in these States. The Princes are watching events in India with close attention, and have declared themselves anxious to keep pace with the advance of self-government in the Provinces, so far as this can be rendered suitable to the needs of their subjects and the conditions which prevail in their dominions. They hold, however, that they ought not to be required, or expected, to embark on artificial reproductions of Western methods and institutions which at present are merely experimental, and of very doubtful value, in British India itself. They object to pressure brought to bear for this purpose, whether it comes, as it generally did in the past, from over-zealous British administrators, or from Indian politicians in a hurry to democratise the East, which is more likely to happen in the future.

These progressive tendencies, as one of the ablest of the newer school of Princes has pointed out, should be subject to the consideration that Western institutions, Western standards, and Western customs are not necessarily suited to countries where rulers and ruled are still dominated, and still bound together, by traditional sentiment. The ancient usages and inherited practices of the Indian States have an intrinsic value of their own, and are certainly not to be thrown over lightly for some shoddy imitation of Western parliamentarism, already under a shade in several Asiatic and European countries.

What India needs, much more than any political changes, is social and economic reform. In that sense it does require to be modernised, to be brought more closely into touch with newer conceptions of intelligent freedom, to shake off the shackles fastened upon it by bigotry and irrational prejudice in the past. Nationalist agitation takes small note of the most urgent problems. Such is the testimony of the greatest Indian writer of our age, Rabindranath Tagore. "Political freedom," he has written recently, "will not give us freedom if the mind is not free." And again:

> "When we talk of Western nationality we forget that the nations there do not have that physical repulsion, one for the other, that we have between different castes. The social habit of mind which impels us to make the life of our fellow-beings a burden to them where they differ from us, even in such a thing as their choice of food, is sure to persist in our political organisation. How, then, can we think that our task is to build a political miracle of freedom upon that quicksand of social slavery?"

The State durbars, or some of them, may claim that while they decline to allow their people to be disturbed by political agitation they are making progress with genuine social reform. In such matters as hygiene, public instruction, and maternity regulation, they are catching up the Provinces, and sometimes show signs of passing ahead of them. No British Indian Government has yet found itself able to impart primary instruction to more than a small fraction of the population. But the Maharaja of Patiala has introduced a system of free and compulsory primary education for all the children in his principality; and the State of Baroda is pledged to the same policy, which has also been accepted for Travancore.

The worst social evil in India is child marriage, with its resulting degradation of widowhood. Until recently the Indian Government has not ventured to legislate against this fertile source of moral and physical deterioration. Some of the Protected States have done so, and have raised the legal age for matrimony to a slightly more tolerable level, without apparently rousing any ill-feeling among their subjects. This most urgent reform can be quietly effected in a principality while British official members of the Viceroy's Council are vainly striving to overcome the opposition to it of the Brahman and Bengali *intelligentsia* in the Legislative Assembly. But the States have opportunities in such matters which the Central Government lacks. It is difficult to frame a remedial measure which must be applied at once to the whole 250,000,000 of British India. A State durbar can try out the experiment, in its own limited area, and among the small population with which it is in intimate contact, with a better chance of success.

# CHAPTER IV

## ANNEXATION AND ALLIANCE

THE East India Company, for the first century and a quarter of its existence, was a trading corporation. Its directors and managers in England had no desire that it should be anything else. They instructed their agents to concern themselves as little as they could with the politics of India, or the affairs of its rulers and governments. It is true that by charter from the Crown the Company was permitted to wage war with non-Christian Powers, and, therefore, to enter into treaties and alliances with them. But this was a licence of which they were slow to avail themselves. All they wanted from the Emperor, and the other Indian Powers, was security for their factories and agents, freedom to trade, and a fair deal, or if possible something more, as against their European rivals.

The imperialist activity of one of these rivals turned the Company's servants into diplomatists and soldiers. The change came about with startling rapidity. The fierce little campaigns between the French and English in the Carnatic plunged the Company into the confused welter of South Indian war and politics. Clive's dispersal of Suraj-ud-Daula's disorderly host at Plassey made them virtual masters of Bengal. This was in 1757. Only sixteen years later, in 1773, came North's Regulating Act, and Warren Hastings' repudiation of the tribute which the Company had been paying to the Moghul Emperor. The British found themselves suddenly committed to the annexation and administration of vast territories, and in close relations with various Indian rulers and governments.

So they entered upon the series of alliances and engagements whereby the Company was able to establish itself as the predominant Power in India. That position it could not have attained by any other means. The Company, even if backed by the whole available force of Britain, could scarcely have prevailed against the united efforts of the chief political and military systems of India. But the native potentates were quarrelling bitterly with one another, and some of them were always glad to have the British on their side. The Company's policy was to ally itself with one "Country Power" against others.

In the first period of alliances the Company hardly understood its own strength. Its attitude towards the Kings and Princes was one of restraint, and sometimes even of humility. At the best it only claimed to treat with them as equals. Parliament and the directors deprecated further entanglements with local politics. The preamble to Pitt's India Bill of 1784 declared that "to pursue schemes of conquest and dominion in India are measures repugnant to the wish, the honour, and the policy of this nation."

The Company, at this time, was weak, and so far from being in a position to appropriate Indian territory it seemed doubtful whether it would be able to hold out against the conquering tide of Mahratta invasion. Warren Hastings, the greatest of our Empire-builders in Asia, restored the British military prestige, and firmly established the Company's control over the Presidency Provinces. Beyond their boundaries his policy was that of the Ring Fence; he made agreements with a number of native Princes who, he hoped, would be strong enough, with British military assistance, to ward off attacks from without. For this reason he preferred to maintain the King of Oudh as an independent sovereign, thinking that his country would act as a buffer against the Sikhs of the Punjab, while the Sikhs themselves would be a barrier against Mohammedan encroachment from the North.

Under Hastings' successors the system of "subsidiary alliances" was built up, and one State after another agreed to pay subsidies or tribute in return for a guarantee of British aid against aggression. The internal sovereignty of the States was not impugned, and even under the Marquess Wellesley, who was bent on consolidating and extending British power, the fiction of equality of status between the contracting parties was observed, so that a formal reciprocity is insisted upon in the treaties. But from Wellesley's *régime* onwards those treaties made it a condition that in return for the Company's protection the States should abandon the right to dispose of their external relations.

Under the succeeding Governors-General the British Government had become the Paramount Power in India, and it had linked itself by a chain of alliances with nearly all the important States, including those left stranded by the final overthrow of the Mahratta combination. Baroda, Scindhia, Holkar were under protection as well as Hyderabad, Mysore, and the Rajput principalities.

The enfeebled situation of these once formidable units tempted active administrators and political agents to reduce them to further dependence. British officials, misled by those European analogies to which reference has already been made, were inclined to insist on their "feudal" relationship to the "suzerain" Power, and to claim an undefined right of intervention in their domestic affairs. Such claims, however, were not formally asserted, and were sometimes formally repudiated, by their authors. Lord Hastings himself explained that a State might pledge itself to "act in subordinate co-operation with the British Government and acknowledge its supremacy," without forfeiting its internal independence.

There was a tendency to respect this qualified autonomy during the great and fruitful period in British-Indian history which lasted until the close of Lord William Bentinck's governorship in 1835. The fine body of statesmen and administrators of that era, men like Tod, Munro, Elphinstone, and Bentinck himself, were more intent on improving and consolidating British

India than in extending its boundaries. They were inclined to leave the native States very much to themselves, though no doubt they thought that their natural destiny was to pass under direct British authority in the fulness of time.

A more impatient temper dominated the councils of Calcutta and Simla during the next twenty years under Lord Auckland (1834–1842), Lord Ellenborough (1842–1844), Lord Hardinge (1844–1848), and Lord Dalhousie (1848–1856). Hard-fought campaigns, sometimes disastrous, but in their general result successful, had confirmed the supremacy of the Paramount Power. Its servants were inclined to resent the moderation of their predecessors in respect to the native States. Able and ambitious men, convinced of the immeasurable benefits of British rule, were in a hurry to extend it, by catching at excuses for intervention or annexation. In 1843 we went to war with the Amirs of Sind and annexed their country, a proceeding which the victorious General, Sir Charles Napier, described as "a very advantageous, useful, and humane piece of rascality." But political rascality is seldom really advantageous; and this transaction set up a feeling of unrest which was increased by our intervention in Gwalior State the following year, when a rebel force was defeated, and a strong British contingent placed in cantonments near Scindhia's capital. In 1849 the Sikhs were finally overthrown and the Punjab was annexed. In 1852 and 1853 Lower Burma was taken from the King of Ava. Then came the denunciation of the Treaty of 1801 with the King of Oudh, his deposition, and the incorporation of his territory in the Lieutenant-Governorship of the North-West (now the United) Provinces.

The Oudh Government was oppressive, corrupt, and feeble; but it had been loyal to the English, and its supersession, in apparent defiance of treaty rights, caused much uneasiness among the Indian Princes and Chiefs. This was further increased by the application of Lord Dalhousie's doctrine of "lapse," under which the suzerain Power held itself entitled, in certain cases, to take over the dominions of a sovereign who died without leaving a natural heir, ignoring, in such an event, the Indian practice of adoption. "Feudalism" might offer some warrant for this action, but it was entirely opposed to Indian law and custom.

The zealous and energetic leaders of the new bureaucracy, which had purged itself of the abuses of the Company's earlier history, felt that they were capable of becoming a kind of earthly providence for all the peoples of India; and the victories gained over Mussulmans, Mahrattas, Sikhs, and other formidable enemies, led them to believe that their power was equal to their will. They were impatient of any jurisdiction in India which might oppose or obstruct their purpose. But unquestionably their high-handed dealing with the native States helped to lay the train which fired the Mutiny of 1857.

# CHAPTER V

## PARAMOUNTCY AND SUBORDINATION

THE British power in India had been established by the aid of Indian rulers; it was saved by their fidelity in the worst crisis of its subsequent history. Throughout the Mutiny, all the more influential among them stood firmly by their engagements, and well it was for us that they did so. If all or several of the greater States had joined the insurrection the British position would have been precarious indeed. But the Nizam, Bhopal, Rajputana, and Central India generally, remained loyal in spite of pressure from their own troops and many of their subjects; the Maharajas of Patiala, Jhind, and Nabha, placed their military contingents at the disposal of the Punjab officers; and our ally, Jang Bahadur of Nepal, marched down with a fine Gurkha army which rendered valuable assistance in the operations before Lucknow.

These services were acknowledged in the post-Mutiny settlement. Queen Victoria's famous Proclamation of November 1, 1858, which transferred the possessions and executive authority of the East India Company to the Crown, declared that no further extension of territory would be attempted or allowed.

"We hereby announce to the Native Princes of India that all Treaties and Engagements made with them by or under the authority of the Honourable East India Company are by Us accepted and will be scrupulously observed; and We look for the like observance on their part. We desire no extension of Our present territorial possessions; and while We will admit no aggression upon Our dominions or Our rights to be attempted with impunity We shall sanction no encroachment on those of others. We shall respect the rights, dignity, and honour of the Native Princes as Our own; and We desire that they, as well as Our own subjects, should enjoy that prosperity and that social advancement which can only be secured by internal peace and good government."

This explicit declaration has been several times confirmed by Queen Victoria's successors, as, for example, in King George's Proclamation of 1921:

"In My former Proclamation (1919) I repeated the assurance, given on many occasions by My Royal predecessors and Myself, of My determination ever to maintain unimpaired the privileges, rights, and dignities of the Princes of India. The Princes may rest assured that this pledge is inviolate and inviolable."

Queen Victoria's Proclamation was followed in 1861 by Lord Canning's issue of *sanads* (grants or letters of recognition) to all the more important States confirming the Princes' right of adoption on the failure of direct heirs. Thus Dalhousie's doctrine of "lapse" was itself allowed to lapse, and it could no longer be maintained that an Indian principality, like a feudal estate, escheated to the Crown if there were no natural heir to the succession.

The era of annexation was definitely closed. The partition of India into British India and Protected India rests on the solemn assurance and pledges of the Imperial Crown. An Indian State could, of course, voluntarily cede part of its territory on lease or otherwise; but the cession could not, without a gross breach of faith, be claimed against its will, either on a demand from the executive government, representing the sovereign, or as the result of any Act or Resolution of a British or British-Indian legislature.

The ban on territorial acquisition has not been violated. So far from seeking opportunities to incorporate Indian States, the British Government has declined them when they may have seemed to offer themselves. The notable instance is that of Mysore, which was, as already mentioned, restored to the rule of the Prince who represented the former reigning family after being for half a century under British control. The Instrument of Transfer contained stringent conditions and regulations which the Maharaja and his successors were expected to observe in the administration of his dominions.*

This rendition of autonomy, even with exceptional limitations, to a State so long in British hands, was highly appreciated in India. It showed that the self-denying clause of Queen Victoria's Proclamation was not a mere form of words. "Now that annexation is at an end," said Scindhia, the Maharaja of Gwalior, "we breathe freely, even when our failings are proved and our shortcomings discussed." But of these failings and shortcomings a good deal was to be made. The statesmen and officials of the later nineteenth century in India did not wish to appropriate State territory. What they did want was influence and supervision. The Princes could feel that their frontiers were safe. But within the frontiers it was assumed, or at any rate hoped, that a constant endeavour would be made to conform to the ideas of their patrons. The "subordinate co-operation" of the Princes was interpreted to mean a close attention to the views and opinions of the Indian Government, and a willing obedience to its mandates.

Protection, to this school of Anglo-British statesmanship, seemed to imply a kind of tutelage. The Paramount Power, in

---

* A more recent example of the restoration of State rights is that of Benares which, after being treated, for more than a century, as a "domain" under the Provincial Government, was, in 1911, reconstituted a State.

virtue of its paramountcy, would exercise a general superinten-
dence over the States and provide that nothing was done against
the interests of India—of which, of course, the Indian Government
was the best judge. This did not mean aggression, but it did mean
intervention and a certain indirect control.

Some of the Princes protested, but as a rule they acquiesced.
They submitted, sometimes rather reluctantly, to the presence of
the privileged and highly placed Resident at their capitals, who
kept a sharp eye on their doings, and was seldom backward with
authoritative advice and peremptory remonstrances.

During the forty years after the Mutiny India appeared to be
politically stabilised. The British Power was supreme. The military
rebellion had been crushed; elaborate and, as it was thought,
sufficient precautions had been taken against overt disaffections
of any kind. India was being ruled, for almost the first time in its
history, mainly for the benefit of its docile and peaceful millions.
The rulers were the most upright and capable body of officials
the world had seen. The task to which these men devoted their
gifts of character and intellect was to keep order among that vast
complex of peoples, so long storm-tossed and war-riven, and to
bring a more secure prosperity and a higher civilisation to the
masses. Such was England's work in Asia, and few doubted that
it was being well done, least of all the men who were doing it.

These energetic, self-confident, somewhat self-opinionated,
administrators looked with a certain impatience on the Native
States. In them they detected too numerous traces of that old
Oriental Adam they were trying to root out. Some of the States
were backward and slovenly, and in those days of reform and
"enlightenment" we were in a hurry to confer on Eastern peoples
the full and latest blessings of Western progress. "We should be
struck," says an Indian historian caustically, "with the absurdity
of blaming Solomon for not establishing a penny post from Dan
to Beersheba; yet some of our Anglo-Indian reformers would

think nothing of disarming a Pathan Chief, and then asking him to subscribe to a dispensary."

This forward school of statesmen and high officials would have liked to see the uniform and systematic methods of our district administration extended to every corner of India. They could not annex the States; but they could convert them to better ways, and intervene to correct their errors when these seemed too grave. The theory of paramountcy or suzerainty was supposed to authorise interference going much further than the control of the military forces and external relations. "If we support you we expect in return good government," said Lord Mayo to the Rajput Chiefs. To ensure such government, the Viceroy's Council in 1867 asserted the right to veto the nomination of a Dewan or Minister in a native State of whom they disapproved.

The assumed analogy of feudalism was pressed far. The Paramount Power not merely required that every succesion to a *gadi* should receive its confirmation. It also enunciated and acted upon the principle that it could assume the control of a State during the minority of a ruler. This practice was encouraged on the ground that it enabled the Government during a minority to organise the administration more or less on the British-Indian model. The officials who conducted affairs during a minority rule were honestly desirous of promoting order and reform. But they could not forget that they were servants of the Government of India; and some of the Chiefs complained that in such matters as the construction of roads and railways and fiscal regulation the interests of that Government were consulted more assiduously than those of the local *régime*.

Another very important right asserted by the Paramount Power after the Mutiny was that of deposing a ruler guilty of misconduct. This was also supported by the fallacious "feudal" analogy. A stronger argument would be that of necessity and the common interest; for the Power which is responsible for the peace and good order of the whole realm cannot look on passively at misrule or misbehaviour carried to dangerous lengths. At what moment the danger point is reached, or is likely to be reached, is decided by the Political and Foreign Department of the Central Government, after consultation with its agents on the spot. No doubt the question may sometimes be referred to the Secretary of State for India at home, though I think as a rule he is content to leave it in the hands of the Viceroy and his advisers.

This right of deposition, and of transferring the sovereignty to some other member of the ruling house, has been infrequently exercised. A conspicuous case was that of Mulhar Rao, the Gaekwar of Baroda, in 1875. He was accused of having tried to poison the Resident, and was put on trial before a special tribunal which included two Indian Princes. The charge against the Maharaja was that the alleged crime would be a breach of loyalty to the Crown, and an act of hostility against the British Government. The judges, however, could not come to a unanimous decision, and the Supreme Government thereupon withdrew the charge of disloyalty, and deposed Mulhar Rao for notorious misconduct and gross misgovernment.

According to Sir Charles Tupper, the author of *Our Indian Protectorate* (1893), which represents the current official view in the latter portion of the nineteenth century, this transaction showed that the Indian Princes had no "right divine to govern wrong." He adds: "While the extensive authority of the Paramount Power and its determination not to permit misgovernment, for which it was indirectly responsible, were thus exhibited, the rulers and chiefs were assured, by the signal fact of the restoration of a native administration, that the desire to avoid further acquisition of territory was perfectly sincere." Sir William Lee-Warner, another great authority, writing from approximately the same standpoint about this time, says that the Baroda deposition was "a public exhibition of the new principle of interference"—that is, presumably, the principle that the Government of India, in virtue of its suzerainty and supremacy, had a general right to check mal-administration and to insist on useful reforms in the Protected States, even if no such right has been reserved by treaty, convention, or *sanad.*

In 1891 occurred the deposition and punishment of the ruler or Jubraj of Manipur. The British Government demanded the expulsion from the State of a person who had raised a rebellion. The Jubraj refused, and the Chief Commissioner of Assam, with an escort, was sent to Manipur to insist on compliance with the Government orders, and treacherously murdered, together with some of his officers. The Jubraj was arrested, tried, and sentenced to death. It was an emphatic assertion of paramount authority; but also an assertion, according to Lee-Warner, of the much more doubtful "right" (which he calls unquestioned) "to remove by administrative order any person whose presence in the State may seem objectionable." But this seems an act of prerogative, justified by necessity, rather than a legal power vested in the Government of India, unless prescribed by treaty or explicit understanding.

Other abdications and transfers of succession have been, from time to time, required, and as a rule they have been quietly accepted. The deposed Prince has usually been quite aware that he has given good cause for his removal, and his subjects have known it also, so that his compulsory retirement is not greatly resented. The British Government is reluctant to call for a Prince's resignation merely on account of a personal offence against morality or propriety, though it will sometimes do so if scandalous misconduct has occurred.

This system of tutelage and close supervision, the application of Lee-Warner's "new principle of interference," was applied with increasing energy by successive Viceroys and their ministers during the later portion of Queen Victoria's reign. They would have liked every State to be as Anglicised in its administration, and as closely tied down by rules and regulations, as Mysore, which was held up as an example of sound native management. They forgot that Mysore was virtually a new State created, or recreated, by the British Government, which had the right to make such conditions as it pleased for its future governance. It stood on a different footing from other States which had never been under British rule, and had been independent kingdoms or principalities when the East India Company sought their alliance.

Anglo-Indian high officialdom was inclined to treat all the "feudatories" alike, and to consider that they really existed on sufferance and ought, in consequence, to defer humbly to the views of the Central Government conveyed to them through the Resident. This theory of unquestioned superiority on the one side, and unquestioning subordination on the other, was pushed to its highest point by Lord Curzon, who held that no Indian ruler could leave India without the permission of the Viceroy. He also seemed to hold that there were no limits to the sovereign prerogatives of the Crown in dealing with Indian States except such as the Crown chose to lay down for itself. It was late in the day to enunciate this uncompromising doctrine (even if it had any legal validity) in an Indian atmosphere beginning to palpitate with a new political self-consciousness at the opening of the nineteenth century.

# CHAPTER VI

## THE PERIOD OF ACQUIESCENCE

In the period of tutelage the Native States were in some ways attractive. Not many tourists visited their capitals, but those who did were usually delighted. It was pleasant to get away from the India of the British, with its big semi-modernised towns, its military and civil stations, its rather aggressively Anglo-Saxon *sahibs,* and its *mem-sahibs,* often too redolent of the suburbs or "the county"—to leave all this for an Asia that was still Asiatic and Oriental. No wonder a romancer, like Pierre Loti, grew enthusiastic over the palaces, the temples, the unspoilt medievalism of the principalities. No wonder other sentimental travellers exclaimed that this was the real India, the India of the picture-books and the legends.

> "Peer into the rows of dim little booths as you pass. Here is the armourer at his work, and the goldsmith, and the man who puts spots and borders of silver tinsel on the cotton saris. The money-changer sits at his door with his scales and measures and little heaps of coin; if you give him a quarter of a rupee, which is four-pence, he will fill both your hands with bits of copper that represent the small currency of the Maharana's realm. A huge Brahminy bull wanders by, none making him afraid, for he can nose into what stalls and baskets he pleases, a licensed plunderer and drone. And here is the man whom the King delights to honour, resplendent in silk and cloth of gold, with his

runners before him to clear the way; here a young cavalier riding down the street with his falcon perched upon his gloved wrist; here a Rajput noble, in helmet and crest, with a hauberk of chain-mail descending over his shoulders, followed by a knot of armed retainers with long spears and rusty scimitars. In the cool of the evening you may see many people walking upon the flat roofs of the houses, even as King David walked when his eye lighted upon the wife of Uriah the Hittite; you may, perchance, come upon Jezebel, with her head tired, looking out from an upper window. We have come far from the world of the twentieth century."

The visitor, not looking below the surface, was tempted to wish that British officialism would just leave these picturesque survivals to go their own way. But the Indian Government and, in fact, the State Governments, too, had other things in mind. What the Maharaja or the Nawab had more particularly to consider was the British Resident, who claimed a good deal of his attention. The Resident is not only the diplomatic envoy of the Protecting Power but also the guardian of British interests and property. The Indian Government has jurisdiction over all persons and things within its military cantonments and civil stations, and likewise over railway lines, forming part of, or continuous with, the general Imperial system. It has, in some States, its own post offices, and must see that its mail and telegraph services are properly conducted. The Resident must also look after the extradition of criminals, and ascertain that Europeans charged with offences are either handed over to the Indian authorities, or are given a fair and proper trial in competent State courts. If the local durbar has anything to say to the Supreme or Provincial Government, or to any other Protected State, it addresses itself to the Resident, who will make the desired communication.

Further, as has been already pointed out, the Resident exercises a general surveillance over the State affairs and reports on them to his superiors. He can offer his "advice" to the ruler on such matters as he thinks fit, and make suggestions as to his Highness' policy and administration. How far he should go in tendering this counsel is a moot point. It shifts according to the personality of the Resident himself, that of the Prince, and those of the Viceroy or Provincial Governor. The advice must be listened to with respect, but a strong and capable ruler may sometimes ignore it, though he does so at his own risk. He may find the diplomatic admonition in due course followed by a demand from headquarters for a change in the personnel or the methods of his administration, with which he is expected to comply.

In the era of tutelage he generally did comply or gave the appearance of doing so. The Princes during this period were reluctant to assert their rights aggressively. They grumbled and sometimes protested, but usually submitted. For this acquiescence there were several reasons, some of which have now lost their force. The Princes were loyal to the Crown, and felt some hesitation in disputing with persons who were supposed to be acting under the Sovereign's orders. Then they were overawed by the strength and majesty of the Paramount Power, which loomed so mysteriously large and acted so vigorously. Who could set himself against the *circar?* It would be discourteous to do so, and might be unsafe. Added to all this was the conviction in the minds of the more intelligent Princes and Chiefs that the Government had some cause for pressing reforms upon them. Their States were, no doubt, retrograde in many respects, and could usefully take lessons from the more advanced Provinces.

Compliance was not always rendered easy by the manner in which it was demanded. The "politicals" of the older school were not invariably tactful. Those directly appointed to the greater States by the Central Government were often men of ability, but the Provincial Governments, which nominated agents to their own groups in the Protectorate, had frequently to fall back on military men who had passed to civil employment, or appoint second-rate members of the bureaucracy who did not expect to qualify for the higher posts in their own service. If these gentlemen happened to be fussy, conceited, or pompous, the machinery did not work smoothly. There was often a tendency among the politicals to deal out a contemptuous patronage to the potentates to whom they were accredited. At times they were openly insolent. King Edward VII., when visiting India as Prince of Wales in 1875, was unfavourably impressed by some of these functionaries. In a letter to Queen Victoria he wrote:

> "What struck me most forcibly was the rude and rough manner with which the English Political Officers (as they are called who are in attendance on native Chiefs) treat them. It is indeed much to be deplored, and the system is, I am sure, quite wrong."

There has been a salutary change of late years. The political agents treat the ruling Princes and Chiefs with respect, and the old bullying tone has been generally dropped. This is sound policy, for the heads of the older dynasties are important personages in India, and they have an influence which may easily be extended beyond their own States. It is a fact ignored by native agitators, and entirely unrecognised in this country; but it exists, and may be noted by any observer who keeps his eyes open. I saw evident signs of it during the Royal visit to India in 1905. I wrote at the time:

> "The head of one of the older and more famous dynasties is undoubtedly a personage even outside his own domin- ions. It was impossible to mingle with the crowd in the cities through which the Prince of Wales passed without feeling that some of these potentates aroused an interest

in the native breast deeper than that evoked by any British official, not excluding the highest of all. A Governor or Lieutenant-Governor, the virtual ruler of thirty or forty millions of people, is in reality a far more important person, especially in his own Province, than any of the local reigning chiefs. Yet I think that the multitude, or some of them, looked on the Maharaja, as he went by in his gilded coach and four, followed by his caracoling escort, with a livelier and more sentimental curiosity than that called forth even by the 'Lord Sahib' himself."

To the Indian natives, our officers, civil and military, our judges, commissioners, generals, commanders-in-chief, provincial satraps, viceroys, are mortal men like themselves; highly placed and highly paid servants, dignified and potent, but evanescent; here to-day and gone to-morrow, moved about at the bidding of unknown masters. It is otherwise with the man who reigns by right of birth. The sacredness of the "Lord's Anointed" is still a living force in the East, though the idea would be expressed differently. Loyalty has much of the old meaning which it has lost in Europe; it includes a sort of religious reverence for the person of the sovereign, and a disposition to regard obedience to his commands as something higher than a legal duty. To those beyond the ranks of his own subjects the Ruling Chief frequently represents something of significance. Even when their material power is trivial these Princes may wield a moral influence sufficient to render their content or discontent with the prevailing system a question worth very serious consideration.

It may be that the Prince, especially if he was of the old school, was not wholly pleased with his lot; but he had some solid grounds for satisfaction. In return for that fidelity to the Imperial Crown, which he found in no way irksome or uncongenial, he was guarded and secure, and defended alike against aggression from without and internal rebellion. His throne was guaranteed to him and his heirs; he could not be thrust from it by hostile invasion or military revolt. So long as he governed with reasonable efficiency the Paramount Power would see that he was not disturbed. He could enjoy his honours and his revenues in peace. He might, if philosophically minded, compare his situation favourably with that of many other rulers in many other lands and ages.

Yet, it had its drawbacks. For one thing he was denied those martial activities which had been the breath of life to his warlike ancestors. Having guaranteed him against attack we saw no need for him to keep any military force at all except for police purposes. Several of the Princes, when they joined the Protectorate, possessed formidable armies, as we had good reason to know. We made it difficult for them to have modern arms and equipment or artillery, so that they could not become really efficient.

I may perhaps be allowed again to reproduce some words I wrote on this subject nearly a quarter of a century ago. Some of the State levees used to make a brilliant appearance, for we exercised no veto upon the sartorial fancies of the Maharaja, and if his Highness chose to clothe his horde of military retainers, armed with smooth-bore muskets and old Enfield carbines, in uniforms of canary yellow, or blue and silver with French dragoon helmets, we did not offer any objection. His subjects liked the show, and were pleased to see these warriors facing about and presenting arms, while Colonel Gopal Singh or Major Mohammed Khan gave the word of command in what was supposed to be the English language. But to a young Prince of spirit the whole affair must doubtless have appeared rather silly and theatrical. Things have changed a good deal in the last twenty-five years, though even these second or third line troops might have been—and may still be—of some military value for operations in India, if ineffective in foreign warfare.

At any rate, a Ruling Prince is not now debarred from serious military activities. He has been allowed to furnish his contribution to the Imperial Service Corps in a businesslike and soldierly way. The Imperial Service Corps was instituted by Lord Dufferin who asked "those Chiefs who have specially good fighting material in their armies to raise a portion of those armies to such a pitch of general efficiency as will make them fit to go into action side by side with Imperial troops." Lord Lansdowne developed the system and placed it on a sound basis. Each unit of the Imperial Service Corps was part of the army of the State, and paid for out of its revenues; the officers were the Prince's own subjects holding their commission from him. The Indian Government required that there should be a British inspecting officer to see that the force was kept up to the standard of our own army. It had modern weapons and received proper instruction in drill and tactics, and was held fit to take its place in line with British troops in the field.

These anticipations were fulfilled when the Great War came. With the lessons of that war in their minds the British authorities have encouraged the development of the Imperial Service troops into the State Forces, now completely under the control of the local governments acting in unison with the higher military command. The old jealousy and suspicion of the native armies has passed away. The State troops are no longer regarded as a potential source of danger to the British power. On the contrary they are esteemed as useful auxiliaries. They can always be called upon for service abroad, and, perhaps, also in India itself if the occasion for their employment should unhappily arise.

# CHAPTER VII

## THE NEW ERA AND THE REVIVAL OF STATE RIGHTS

THE close of the Curzon viceroyalty in 1905 marks the end of the period of tutelage and subserviency. New currents were stirring the Indian air in the early years of the present century, and they grew in strength until they gained a fresh and more vivid impulse from the War. India was becoming awake and sensitive. The comparative calm of the later Victorian age was broken by a furious agitation, crossed by perceptible elements of conspiracy and seditious violence, not checked nor stayed by earnest legislative efforts to enlarge the political liberties of the Indian peoples.

The new spirit in British India, both among the governors and the governed, had its repercussion in the Protected area. When the policy was avowed of preparing the Provinces by gradual stages for responsible government it was no longer possible to maintain the old attitude of domination towards the States. They also, it was recognised, had a considerable part to play in the new Indian scheme of things. Moreover, it seemed that the Paramount Power, instead of regarding the principalities as a potential source of danger, might have to rely upon their assistance in time of trouble. The Princes were unquestionably, and even enthusiastically, loyal, as they were to show in the Great War, when they showered profuse offers of men, money, aeroplanes, and munitions upon the Imperial Government. The fidelity and tranquillity that prevailed in the States contrasted with the turmoil in some of the provincial centres of population.

The vice-regal speeches from 1905 onwards emphasised the

policy of cordial co-operation rather than that of patronage and intrusive surveillance. "I have made it a rule," said Lord Minto in 1909, "to avoid the issue of general instructions as far as possible, and have endeavoured to deal with questions as they arose with reference to existing treaties, the merits of each case, local conditions, antecedent circumstances, and the particular stage of development, feudal and constitutional, of individual principalities." He took occasion to give a significant admonition to over-officious Residents.

> "The foundation stone of the whole system is the recognition of identity of interests between the Imperial Government and the Durbars and the minimum of interference with the latter in their own affairs. ... I can assure political officers I am speaking in no spirit of criticism. My aim and object will be, as it always has been, to assist them, but I would impress upon them that they are not only the mouthpiece of Government and the custodian of Imperial policy, but that I look to them also to interpret the sentiment and aspirations of the Durbars."

There was also a recession from the old policy of keeping the States in isolation, and forbidding their rulers to have any intercourse with one another. On the contrary the Viceroys encouraged them to confer together and consulted them collectively. It took them into a kind of partnership on matters of general interest, and this attitude was emphasised during the War by the Imperial Government, which invited Indian Princes to meetings of the Cabinet in London, and the Imperial Conference. In 1918–1919 the Maharaja of Bikaner attended the European Peace Conference and was one of the signatories of the Treaty of Versailles.

The revived political importance of the Protected States found its echo in the Montagu-Chelmsford Report on Indian

Constitutional Reforms. This document recognised that the Princes had a claim to be consulted on matters which concerned the States as well as British India. It was suggested that there should be a Council or Chamber of Princes with a small Standing Committee, to which the Political Department of the Government of India might refer questions affecting the States, and arrange for joint deliberation on questions of common interest. In January, 1919, the proposal was considered in a Conference of the Ruling Princes held at Delhi. There was much difference of opinion as to whether all the States, or only those possessing full powers, should be represented. On this point no agreement was reached, and it urgently calls for settlement; for it is obvious that the numerous petty baronies, whose rulers have agreed to resign some of the main functions of independent government, cannot be put on the same footing as the large autonomous units.

The Conference, however, agreed to the institution of a House of Princes (Narendra Mandal). The Princes' suggestions were endorsed, with some modifications, by the Secretary of State for India and the Viceroy (Lord Chelmsford). The Chamber of Princes was constituted and formally inaugurated by the Duke of Connaught in February, 1921. It has an elected Chancellor (now the Maharaja of Patiala, who has succeeded the Maharaja of Bikaner) and an elected Standing Committee of six members, which is understood to discuss questions touching State rights and interests, such as posts, telegraphs, and railways, in both British and native territory, with the Foreign and other departments of the Central Government. The Chamber meets annually, and so far its proceedings have been private. Whether all Ruling Princes should have the right to attend, or only some of them, still remains open for decision. At present there are 108 full-powered members of the Chamber, and 12 representatives for 120 smaller States.

The creation of the Chamber of Princes marks a stage in the adjustment of the relations between the Protectorate and the

Paramount Power, but can hardly be the final stage. The State durbars are not yet satisfied. While grateful for the ampler recognition accorded to them during the past twenty years they still think that they are entitled to something more. They hold that they should be assigned a definite place in any new system of Indian policy which may be considered by Parliament when the Report of the Simon Commission is presented.

This body is not the only one which has been inquiring into Indian constitutional and political problems. It deals with the conditions in British India only; it cannot, and ought not, to frame a constitution for the whole of "India" without reference to the status and needs of the non-British area and population. Alongside the Statutory (Simon) Commission another set of authoritative investigators has been at work. This was the Indian States Committee, with Sir Harcourt Butler as President, appointed to examine the rights, duties, and legal position of the Protected States.

The Statutory Commission attracted abundant attention in Great Britain, partly because of the personal and political reputation of its leading member, partly because of the publicity given to its proceedings, and partly through the efforts of native agitators who have advertised it by vociferous meetings and disorderly demonstrations. On the other hand, the Butler Committee was scarcely noticed. It met unobtrusively in a room in a London Government office to which neither the public nor the press was admitted. It is safe to say that not one British elector in a thousand heard of its existence. But its importance cannot be overlooked. The future destinies of India cannot be determined with reference to the 247 millions of the Provinces alone. The 72 millions of the Protected area must also, in one way or another, be brought into the scheme if it is to have effectiveness and permanence.

The Butler Committee went to work under terms of reference accepted by the Committee of the Princes, who for several years had asked that their position should be investigated. This insistent pressure is typical of the revived self-consciousness of the Protected potentates during the present century. They are no longer in the same mood of placid acquiescence as their pre-decessors of the post-Mutiny generation. These were inclined to submit rather humbly to the mandates of the Residents and the Central Government. They felt their own weakness in face of the Power which had stamped out the rebellion, and were not eager to dispute its decrees. Deprived of the control of military and diplomatic affairs, they had never been trained in the hard school which had given the native communities such energetic leaders in the past. All they asked for was a quiet life without the friction which might have arisen if they had sought to vindicate their own rights with vigour. Besides, they were rather ignorant, and in the hands of advisers imperfectly acquainted with English mentality and English law.

Their successors are better equipped. During minority regen-cies, and in various other ways, we have stimulated instruction in the princely families. The Ruling Chief of to-day is usually well educated and alert. He has probably been trained at a college or university under English tutors and professors, he speaks our language perfectly, reads our books and newspapers, travels in Europe, and knows a great deal more about us than we do about him. He has studied our politics, followed our parliamentary debates, and understands who the rulers of British India are and where they stand in the estimation of their countrymen. He has called well-informed and capable men, English or Indian, to his councils, and has given a close scrutiny to the contracts and agree-ments which define his position.

He is more loyal to the Empire than his fathers, and he un-derstands and appreciates Western culture and progress as they did not. But he is likewise much more inclined to think for himself. The contrast between the British-ruled Provinces and his own dominions can no longer be presented to him with the same conviction. In the past he might be invited to compare his State, still rather primitive and barbaric, with the British districts, well ordered, peaceful, and moving steadily onward. In the light of our recent experiences, an astute Prince might turn the argument the other way round. "In our territories," he might say, "high personages and officials need not go about in fear of assassination. We do not see turbulent mobs assembling in our cities which have to be dispersed by bayonets and rifles. We are not required to be on guard against chronic conspiracy; nor are there persons in our midst who were secretly trafficking with the enemy during the War, and are still subsidised by aliens who seek to overthrow the Empire. Our subjects are apparently less discontented than yours and like our methods of government better." The British-Indian official might reply that this was not quite the whole of the matter; but he would have to admit that there was something in it, and would no longer contend, as some of his predecessors did, that it would be an unquestionable benefit for the States to become British Provinces, in effect, if not in name.

As the sittings of the Butler Committee were secret, no disclosure was authorised of the detailed statement laid before it on behalf of the Council of Princes. This was drawn up by some of the most distinguished members of the English Bar, and at the time of writing it has not been made public. Meanwhile, we know pretty well, from their own speeches and other announcements, what are the main points in the Princes' case. Primarily, they urge that their relationship with the British Government is determined by the treaties, and cannot legally be put on any other basis. Neither usage, convention, nor theories based on paramountcy or suzerainty can annul the contract made between a State and the British Crown, represented by the East India Company or the Viceroy in Council. Like other agreements, it can only be modified by the assent of the contracting parties.

Further, the Princes object to the extension of the term "subordinate co-operation" into virtual subjection, as maintained by Sir Charles Tupper, and, in a less degree, by Sir William Lee-Warner, and other official and semi-official publicists. Their territories, they urge, are sovereign States. There can be no question that they were so recognised in the earlier treaties of alliance, and it does not appear that the status has been generally forfeited. This was distinctly asserted by a great Indian ex-Viceroy, who is also a great lawyer, no longer ago than on December 4, 1928. On that date, Lord Reading, in the House of Lords, referred to the Protected units as "the sovereign States," and deprecated "changing the sovereignty which the Princes at present enjoyed." The States have sovereign powers except in so far as they have agreed to surrender part of those powers in return for protection and security.

The extent of the surrender is determined for each State by its fundamental treaty, *sanad,* or understanding. In some of the minor lordships it has been extensive. In the important group it has been limited to the control of external relations and defence. The States are semi-sovereign, if I may thus briefly dismiss a great juristic controversy, except in so far as this limitation goes. They have handed over to the Governor-General of India their liberty to conduct their foreign policy in return for security against aggression and insurrection. The obligation is that of protection on one side and fidelity to the Empire and the Crown on the other. Beyond this there may be a number of other rights transferred to the Government of India, such as those giving it jurisdiction over resident British subjects, and over railway stations, cantonments, and telegraph offices; but these, it is contended by the Princes, must be the subject of special arrangements, and are not covered by the general terms of protection.

The Princes, I believe, complain that the treaties and agreements have frequently been interpreted to their disadvantage by the agents of the Paramount Power, who have insisted on concessions connected with fiscal, economic, and transport matters, not authorised by the contracts and extorted by a pressure which cannot be resisted. They may protest, but their protest can only go before the Central Government, which is, through one or other of its departments, an interested party in the dispute. If it decides in favour of its own agents, the aggrieved durbar has no redress. Thus it may be compelled to agree to (and perhaps pay for) the construction of a branch line which may be useful to the general railway system of India, though of no value to the State concerned.

The principalities being, as a rule, poorer and less fertile than the Provinces, have lagged behind in the industrial movement. But they maintain that their progress would have been more substantial if they had been given a fairer chance. The fiscal, customs, and excise policies of the Indian Government are conceived in the interests of the British-Indian majority, not in those of the Protected minority. The States are mostly inland districts with practically no access to the sea except through British territory. Duties may be levied on foreign imports which accrue to the Indian revenue, while the people of the States have to pay more for their goods without any corresponding benefit to the local treasuries. At the instance of the Swarajists the Indian Legislature has imposed a tariff on imported steel. The tax falls mainly on Indian consumers by a rise in prices, including, of course, those in the Protected States; but these States do not receive a rupee from the proceeds of this impost. The duty, which hits the British manufacturer, as it happens, as well as the native States, is settled without the assent of the latter, solely in the assumed interests of British India and at the instance of British-Indian politicians.

The advocates of the principalities urge that this is an unfair arrangement and ought not to be perpetuated. In a self-determining India, they say, our 72,000,000 should not be left helpless at the mercy either of the officials or the agitators. Our voice, too, ought to be heard, and some constitutional scheme should be evolved so that our views can be expressed with authority and effect.

These are the opinions which, doubtless, were laid before the Butler Committee by Sir Leslie Scott and his learned colleagues. The Committee's Report should come before Parliament, together with that of the Simon Commission, and the reorganisation and reconstruction of the Indian system can only take place after a consideration and comparison of both documents.

# CHAPTER VIII

## THE STATES AND THE PAST

In their present stage of self-conscious co-operation, which has succeeded the passivity and acquiescence era, the State rulers are examining the past and looking towards the future. In the first instance, they are seeking what may be called a redress of grievances. They urge that they have submitted, through weakness, or ignorance, or a salutary respect for the Paramount Power, to substantial infringements upon their contractual rights. Numerous concessions, some of them highly detrimental to their own interests and those of their subjects, have been extracted from them.

Some I have already mentioned, such as those dealing with customs, railways, and extra-territorial jurisdiction. Others are being brought forward. It is complained that States which have never agreed to give up their full powers are treated as mere "feudatories." The feudal analogy, as I have pointed out, is incorrect when applied to the Protected States in general ; though no doubt a certain number of the smaller lordships did stand in a certain relation which might be called that of feudal subordinates to greater Powers such as the Peshwar and the Moghul Emperor, or paid tribute to them. When we occupied the place of these suzerains we acquired such rights as they could claim over their dependents. It does not seem that we are entitled to place on the same footing States which had never been in this position.

If there is a disputed succession in a State, the Indian Government steps in as arbiter, and its award is final. When the succession passes to a minor, the State is placed under a regency, either established in accordance with the State Constitution, or, in default, appointed by the British Government, to conduct the administration till the Prince comes of age. Advantage is taken of this minority rule to put public affairs into good order and to introduce useful reforms. This is often beneficial to the people of the State, as was shown conspicuously in the case of Mysore, which emerged from its long administration under British guidance in admirable condition. But the Princes argue that a minority ought not to be made the occasion for handing over to the Central Government rights, privileges, or cessions of territory, which would probably not have been agreed to by a competent native ruler. Nor ought there to be too much effort to Anglicise the political or administrative methods which may suit the local conditions better than those preferred by zealous bureaucrats anxious to see all India brought into a symmetrical uniformity.

To what extent and on what occasions should the Central Government intervene to direct or influence the internal policy of a State? That is a point on which there is considerable difference of opinion. Some scope for intervention must be admitted. When a Protected ruler governs his dominions so badly as to become a nuisance to his neighbours, or to provoke his subjects to insurrection, the Government of India must act. It is obviously empowered, and even compelled, to do so by its responsibility for the defence, security, and general good order of the States, since it has taken over the control of their military and external policy. It cannot look on passively while a community is falling into chaos, or clearly going the way to render itself an unruly member of the Indian family of nations.

It is, however, suggested that this license to intervene has often been used immoderately or unnecessarily. It ought to be limited, it is urged, to clear cases of gross misgovernment such as might involve the dangers specified. It has been carried much further. The Political Department and its agents have sometimes assumed that as the representatives of the Paramount Power they can exercise a general supervision over the durbars, and insist upon such reforms and remedial measures as they think proper. Very often these demands spring from a sincere desire to promote the welfare of the Protected peoples, and to root out palpable abuses, such as were *suttee,* slavery, torture, and other practices repugnant to humanity and civilised ideas. Sometimes they are inspired by less admirable motives, including the intelligible anxiety of the Central or Provincial Governments to gain advantages for the inhabitants of British India even at the expense of the States.

Good or bad, it is contended, such remedial measures should be obtained by negotiation and arrangement, not by mandate. The Government of India has no legal authority to ask from a State more than the State has agreed to give. It ought not to issue commands as from a superior to a subordinate which must be obeyed because it cannot be resisted. It should not abridge liberties or privileges, which it has bound itself to respect, by the issue of a *sanad,* decree, or affirmation of policy, or an official tender of "advice," which is virtually an order. It may be desirable that a State should not be allowed to hang its own criminals or catch its own elephants. But if it has never expressly abandoned those prerogatives it does not see why it should resign them to meet the views of British-Indian civilians who distrust the native judicature or may be interested in big-game preservation.

The present attitude of the Princes raises the whole question of what is meant by paramountcy in India, an awkward question which it might be more convenient to leave open but which must, I am afraid, be elucidated and disposed of now that it has been authoritatively propounded. Some of the Viceregal Councils of the last century, and their literary supporters, seem almost to have accepted the theory that paramountcy, combined with usage, had conferred on the Government of India a power only limited by its own discretion. It was itself the judge of what it could or could not do, it decided what it pleased, and its decisions were to be regarded as statements of the law which would over-ride or cancel out contractual obligations. Thus, Sir William Lee-Warner:

> "Express conventions among contracting parties must always command a solemn respect, although it is very important to observe that they are subject to the fretting action of consuetudinary law. The decisions of British Courts of Law interpret the provisions of Acts of Parliament; and by a similar process the judgments of the British Government upon issues raised by its dealings with the native States test the Treaties by the touchstone of practical application."*

The Princes deny all this. To the "fretting action of consuetudinary law" they oppose the plain words of Queen Victoria's Proclamation of 1858:

> "We hereby announce to the Native Princes of India that all Treaties and engagements with them by or under the authority of the Honourable East India Company are by Us accepted and will be scrupulously observed, and We look for the like observation on their part."

To this declaration the States hold. They contend that the relationship between them and the Supreme Government is based on definite agreements which are valid unless *both* parties consent to annul or modify them. To withdraw or revise them at the will of one of the partners alone would be an unfair employment of the prerogative. It would be an extra-legal proceeding, what lawyers call an Act of State, or, in other words, an act of force, which may be justified by political necessity but would not be in accordance with the principles we profess to follow, and would be inconsistent with the system we have established.

We have created the greatest Empire the world has known

---

* Lee-Warner, *The Protected Princes of India*, chap. ii.

with little or no liking for imperialism. From what this term implies, we have, from the outset, done our best to keep as far away as possible in India. In that area we have been so clearly dominant that we could have done what we pleased. We might have said, as probably other European nations in a similar position would have said: "We *are* the Paramount Power, and we propose to use our supremacy as seems good to us. We shall rule all India, for its own benefit, of course, but in the manner that we think expedient, and we cannot be hampered by treaties, agreements, or legal fetters of any kind. For we are here by right of conquest and, as conquerors, we are under no restrictions, except such as we choose to impose upon ourselves. As to that, we are the sole judges. You must take what we give you, because we are not really bound to give you anything at all."

We did, however, act quite differently. We did not set out to conquer India, and have never done so. The East India Company—the point will stand repetition—wanted customers, not subjects; it found that the best way to get them was by means of alliance and understanding with the native Powers and sovereigns, and, if it had been possible, it would have been content to enter into such arrangements with all of them. Circumstances compelled us to take over the larger part of the territory and govern it directly. But we did not extinguish native sovereignty in the remainder of the country. We might have done that after 1803, or, at any rate, after 1818, or after 1858. But we preferred to cling to the principle we had avowed of leaving these local governments to co-operate with us under the agreements we had made with them.

That has been our policy, and it shows a respect for justice, a regard for the rule of law over the rule of might, for which I think we deserve more credit than is always allowed us. The Indian Princes are grateful for our forbearance, and they must recognise how much they owe to it and the security we have given them. Generally they do. They appreciate what they have gained through their association with the Imperial Crown, and they do not want this relationship to be altered. It is mainly because they are afraid it *may* be altered to their detriment that they are alive to alleged encroachments on their contractual rights, and ask that these should be investigated, with special reference to approaching possible changes in the Indian constitution. For the political system of India is, or may soon be, in the melting-pot; no one can tell what new form may be given to it during the next few years. It is impossible to foresee how the various powers and authorities which control the machinery may be adjusted and balanced. Incalculable forces are in movement, and we do not know how far they will be permitted to exert pressure, or in what direction.

With all this uncertainty in the political atmosphere, it is essential to have the rights and obligations of the Protected States clearly defined, not only in their own interests, but in those of the whole aggregate. A reconstitution of India, which ignored the principalities or left them with a permanent sense of injury, would be built on shifting sands. British India and Native India are too intimately related to be treated without reference to one another.

# CHAPTER IX

## THE STATES AND THE FUTURE

THE protests of the Princes, representing their State durbars and peoples, against undue interference by the Central Government refer to the past. But I think they are rather made with an eye to the future. They are aimed at dangers which may develop out of the present trend of events in India.

This may account for the anxiety of the State rulers to define the limits of legitimate intervention in their internal concerns. They are more impatient of such obtrusion than they used to be, and for intelligible reasons which have been succinctly and clearly summarised by the Marquess of Reading. "Under the Government of India Act (said the ex-Viceroy), the Princes' affairs were dealt with by the Governor-General in Council, and it was largely because of this that some difficulties had suggested themselves to the Princes. They were alarmed at the notion that they might find themselves dealing with a Governor-General in a Council which was composed of the Governor-General and *Ministers responsible to the Legislative Assembly*"—in other words, with an Indian Government chosen by an Indian electorate.

This is the essence of the matter. The Princes disliked interference from the Central Government, but they could tolerate it when that Government was British. The heads of the Foreign and Political Department, the Viceroys and Lieutenant-Governors and Chief Commissioners, and the Residents and Agents, were Englishmen with English traditions. They might sometimes have been ill-informed, officious, or arrogant, but, on the whole, they were fair-minded and honest, and they had no temptation to be anything else. The local rulers could trust, if they did not always love, these functionaries. They felt that the Government was in the hands of men who were generally capable and upright, and who acted in the interests of all Indians, as they understood them, not in those of a section, class, or community. In these officials, the servants of the British Crown, to which they were bound by treaty, the State rulers felt a confidence which they would not extend to any collection of Indian politicians.

None of the schemes put forward by the various Congress groups inspires them with a sense of security. Of late these bodies have been disputing among themselves as to whether they shall inscribe Independence on their programme or be content, for the present, with Dominion status. Pandit Motilal Nehru, the leader of the Nationalist party in the Legislative Assembly, stands by the latter proposal as the immediate objective. This is the idea of a constitution outlined in the "Nehru Report." It has been vehemently opposed by Mr. Srinavasa Iyengar and his "Independence League," which asks for complete separation from the Empire. As the two parties could not agree, Mr. Gandhi used his great influence in order to get the "All-India National Congress" to adopt what is called a compromise, which may rather be described as a stay of execution. The Congress approves the Nehru scheme of Dominion Government, provided it is accepted by the British Parliament *within twelve months.* If it is not accepted in that space of time the united party will resume the agitation for complete independence.

Both alternatives have left the Protected Princes out of the calculation. But if ever either scheme passes beyond the stage of loose talk it will be seen that they cannot be passed over. In fact, they may be said to dominate the situation, for without their concurrence and consent one project becomes utterly impracticable, and the other is surrounded by almost insurmountable difficulties.

An independent India is a futile dream. There are a score of reasons why it cannot be made a reality. One of them would be quite conclusive if there were no other. This is the character, size, population, geographical location, and military capacity of the principalities. An Indian republic, ruled by a native Cabinet and deprived alike of a British Central executive and a British and British-led Indian Army, would not command the obedience of the States, and it would exist only as long as they thought proper to allow it to remain in being.

There is a hackneyed story which has been got off upon most English inquirers into Indian politics at one time or another. It is the alleged report of a conversation between an August Personage and one of the chiefs of a famous Rajput dynasty. "Tell me, Maharaja Sahib, what would happen if we [the British] left India to-morrow?"

"If you left India to-morrow, Sir, on the day *after* to-morrow my men would be on horseback, and a month after that there would not be a rupee or a virgin left in all Bengal."*

This example of ancient wisdom has a certain appositeness which may excuse its reproduction. Modern Indian Princes are not at all like the Pindarri raiders of the old lawless days, and their subjects are mostly peaceful cultivators. But we cannot ignore the latent element of force which underlies all politics, nor can constitutions be framed in complete disregard of those awkward sciences, geography and ethnology. It does happen to be a fact that the Princes occupy the strategic highlands of India from which they could inundate the plains, as their predecessors used to do; also that a very large proportion of the so-called fighting races—Mahrattas, Sikhs, Rajputs, Northern Mohammedans, and others—are within their territories or just outside their borders. There might be some more vivid pages added to that unfinished chapter of Indian history which was broken off short by Lake,

---

* Miss Kathleen Mayo, in *Mother India*, ingenuously quotes this well-worn tale as a new one conveyed to her at first hand! I printed it myself in my *Vision of India* over twenty years ago, and even then it was of respectable antiquity.

Wellesley, Lord Hastings, and our other military leaders and militant statesmen in the early nineteenth century. We do not care to dwell upon these points in connection with modern Indian politics, though it is still undeniably true that their further peaceful evolution would be hopeless if British bayonets were withdrawn.

That is a contingency which can be left out of account for the present. There will be no immediate occasion for the chivalry of Rajasthan to get into the saddle, or for the Nepal Gurkhas to sharpen their kukris. The British bayonet will not fade out of the picture for a long time to come. We are not going to "leave India" to-morrow, or for very many morrows. Until there has been a complete change, not merely in the Indian situation, but in the world situation, we must keep armies, British and British-controlled, in the great territory we are bound to defend against aggression from without and internal chaos. For since we have largely deprived the Indian peoples of the power to protect themselves we must continue to safeguard them effectually. That is a solemn obligation binding upon the Imperial Crown, by which is meant, of course, the King-in-Council, the Sovereign of Great Britain, acting by the advice of Ministers responsible to the British Parliament.

Nor can that same authority abandon the supreme control of the Indian executive without a grave breach of trust. For it is the guardian of the Indian minorities, who rely upon it to shelter them against oppression or encroachment upon their rights. One minority is that of the 50,000,000 or 60,000,000 of the depressed classes, the "untouchables," who have the strongest objection to being left at the mercy of a Brahman-led legislature and administration. And another minority is that of the 72,000,000 of the Protected States, who claim that no changes should be made in the Indian constitutional system which would place them in a worse position than they are at present. Here is a trust which the Crown has accepted, by treaty, grant, and convention, and it cannot abandon or delegate it against the wishes and interests of those concerned.

This might be done without going so far as to make India "independent" in the sense understood by the extreme Nationalists. The Princes are not particularly alarmed by this threat. In an India turned loose from the British Empire they could take care of themselves. In an India still within that Empire, but left too unreservedly under the direction of a native government, depending upon the majority vote of the British-Indian constituencies, they might be subjected to more dangerous pressure.

This pressure might be both political and economic. On the political side a "democratic" Indian ministry, in control of an Indian legislature, might strive by direct action and persistent propaganda to extend its methods to the principalities. The States, it might insist, must also share in the full benefits of democracy and self-determination, as conceived by advanced Indian politicians. The Princes would be asked to reform their government on these lines. As a fact, as I have shown above, most of them have already gone far in the direction of constitutionalism, and have rather closely followed the British-Indian administrative model, and in social reform some of them have gone beyond the Provinces.

They are prepared to go further, to give their peoples a larger share in the government, and to keep abreast of the extension of popular liberties in British India, so far as the circumstances of their States permit. But they do not want to be forced into a slavish imitation of any system which may be introduced into British India without regard to the real interests and inclinations of their subjects. They are not convinced that a bad adaptation of Western parliamentary models is the best means of rendering an Asiatic population contented, stable, or even free. The State durbars believe that they can raise the social and material level of their peoples much more effectually if they are not forced into precipitate and ill-conceived constitutional innovations.

An Indian Government could not, of itself, put such compulsion on them. But it might be supported from outside. There are ardent reformers in Great Britain already turning a suspicious eye upon Indian "absolutism." Of this there was more than a hint in the remarks of at least one influential speaker during the debate in the House of Lords to which reference has already been made. After observing that "the independent rulers of the Indian States had shown themselves aware of the possibility of their positions, interests, and customs being materially changed, and they had indicated that in any development of the constitution of India they must not be placed under the control of an elected assembly to which they did not contribute, and, further, that they did not desire any alteration of the present relations and responsibilities between themselves and the Crown," he went on to say: "Most, if not all, of the principalities were arbitrary governments. Everything depended on the autocratic will of the sovereign. When the whole framework of Indian Government was being reconstituted, and they were considering how far Indian States could be fitted into that framework, he thought it would be impossible to disregard the question whether the autocratic power of the Princes should not, in some degree, be restricted."

It sounds innocent, but as Lord Reading pointed out, the passage did "give indications that might disturb the Princes very much." Naturally, they do not like the idea of "the framework of Indian Government" being reconstructed according to the plan drawn out by the leaders of the Nationalist party in Delhi, which might, perhaps, receive the support of sympathetic friends in Westminster.

Apart, however, from direct or indirect political action, an Indian Government and legislature could, if unfettered, work grave injury to the States by economic and fiscal measures. The Princes maintain that already they have sometimes been unfairly treated in these matters. The discrimination against them might be carried further. It would be perfectly easy to arrange a tariff, or impose duties, in British India which would weigh heavily on the principalities and impede their industrial development. Consequently, they urge that they should have some voice in the determination of any policy which would affect the peoples and industries of India as a whole.

These are considerations which should be borne in mind when it is proposed to turn India into a self-governing Dominion. To many of us that seems to be the eventual destiny of the great Dependency. It is indeed the goal to which the Montagu-Chelmsford Report pointed; and the Government of India Act was supposed to be one stage towards this conclusion. The idea is in itself attractive. Why not complete the Commonwealth of Nations by this magnificent addition? Side by side with the Dominion of Canada, the Dominion of Australia, the Dominion of South Africa, might be ranged this other Dominion, so much more splendid by its population, its resources, its historic past, than any of them.

India may, in due course, become a Dominion; but it will be a Dominion very different in character and organisation from the others. We cannot, by a stroke of the pen, or any number of strokes, set up an enlarged copy of the Canadian or the Australian constitution in Delhi, nor can we follow the precedent laid down in the creation of the Irish Free State. Many Irish Nationalists resented the exclusion of the Ulster counties. It was, indeed, a somewhat clumsy and cumbrous expedient. But the device was practicable; it can work. Let us, however, try to imagine an Irish Free State, mainly Catholic, with a Protestant Ulster not con-fined to the north-eastern corner but spread out all over Ireland, reaching from the Liffey to the mouth of the Shannon, stretching deep into Munster and Connaught. Let us assume that one strong block of sturdy Orange population would look down from the mountains upon Cork, and another would be planted within an easy march of Dublin. We cannot have an Indian Free State with an Ulster of that kind, an Ulster with 72,000,000 of people, and 700,000 square miles of territory.

An Indian Dominion would be an abortive failure from the outset, and could hardly come into being at all, unless it were provided with some elaborate political machinery, not yet invented, for coping with these unique topographical and ethnical conditions, and for safeguarding the rights and liberties of the communal and other minorities. How this is to be done within the Dominion "framework" remains to be demonstrated, if demonstration be possible. We shall, perhaps, hear more on this question when the reports of the Simon Commission and the Butler Committee come up for discussion in Parliament. It may then be considered how a genuinely democratic system can be reconciled with such an obviously non-democratic principle as communal representation, which is imperative if the minorities are not to be placed in subjection to an oligarchy of the higher caste Hindus. It may also be explained how peace, progress, and good order could be secured if an Indian "Dominion" Government were given the full powers exercised by the central executive and legislature in the other Imperial Commonwealth and Unions.

How we shall deal with these and cognate problems cannot be foreshadowed. I do not know, nor does anybody else, what proposals will be brought before Parliament for the amendment, revision, or annulment of the experiment begun in 1919. It depends not only on the opinions of Sir John Simon, Sir Harcourt Butler and their colleagues, but also on those of whatever Imperial Cabinet may be in office when the next India Bill is brought in. Perhaps there may be a bold and even startling programme; perhaps one that will be merely tentative and cautious. We shall see.

I am more than doubtful, for the reasons above stated, whether real Dominion Government can be adopted for India as a whole. The signs and guide-marks seem to point to something different. I think the obvious destiny of India is Federalism in some form. India is too large to be treated as a single political unit, and so, indeed, are some of the Provinces. Such unwieldy agglomerations as Bengal, Madras, the United Provinces, Bihar, Bombay, and the Punjab, with populations of over 20,000,000, 30,000,000, and 40,000,000, will be subdivided. In the process it may be possible to readjust boundaries so as to make them correspond rather more closely with racial and religious divisions. For this purpose it may be possible to arrange for exchanges of territory between the Provinces and the principalities. This will reduce, if it does not wholly eliminate, the difficulty of communal representation. India will then be apportioned among a large number of Native States and British Provinces of manageable size, each self-governing within its own area, except for military and foreign affairs, and such common matters as posts, telegraphs, and tariffs on oversea imports. I believe the aim will be to allow these units the fullest measure of freedom in their internal government and local finances, unimpeded by any such clumsy apparatus as the dyarchy, which is mainly a source of irritation and inconvenience. The States will have nothing to do with it, and the Provinces would be better without this clog on their responsibility and freedom of action.

I do not see how such an extension of local autonomy can be combined, under the conditions which prevail in India, with a sovereign federal legislature. For the reasons already given there cannot be a full-powered Indian Parliament. The powers of the Council of State and the Legislative Assembly are more likely to be curtailed than extended. The supreme executive must remain with the Crown through its representative, the Governor-General; and I hold, on grounds which have been set forth in the preceding pages, that it cannot properly discharge its trust to all the Indian peoples if it must always act on the advice of a native Ministry.

It ought to have authoritative advice on subjects which touch the common welfare and affect the interests of more than one of the Indian communities. This need will be met by some provisions for joint consultation and impartial decision. Amateur constitution-making is an unprofitable task, and I am not presumptuous enough to attempt it; but I think that some machinery will be devised for enabling the real controlling forces in India to work together in unity. Questions will arise which may be viewed differently by the representatives of the British Empire, by those of the British-Indian populations as a whole, and by those of the peoples of the States. These can only be adjusted fairly between the three parties by conference and agreement.

As regards the States, the Memorandum laid before the Simon Commission by the European Association of India may give some suggestions for a settlement on these lines. It is proposed that to the Provinces should be delegated such powers as would enable each Province individually to deal with social reform. Here the Central Government should not interfere. "The moral and material progress of the peoples is largely dependent on the ability to modify existing and ancient customs to suit the requirements of modern India."

"To ensure an equal advance of public opinion throughout India is a difficult task likely to delay social reforms. Already certain Indian States, possessing as they do the necessary authority, have introduced social reforms, and if Provinces were similarly empowered to undertake social legislation advance would be more rapid, and the consideration of questions of social reform might assist in the healthy growth of parties in the Provincial legislatures."

The Association looks towards "the ultimate and distant goal of an All-India Government, consisting of a federation of Indian States working harmoniously with British India through legislatures which would draw their representatives both from British India and the Indian States." As a step towards this result, which may be "ultimate" but must be extremely remote, there might be built up a federation, or combination of the States, working through the Chamber of Princes, and meeting the Viceroy in a Council to which certain definite powers might be delegated by the individual States. It would be a sort of Governor-General's Council for the principalities, and would be a counterpart to his Executive Council for British India.

The two Councils would meet in joint session to confer on matters affecting both British India and the States. Any decisions reached would be followed by the requisite legislation or executive action by the British-Indian and State Governments. There might also be established a Supreme Court, to the jurisdiction of which the States would become amenable, and to which controversies between them and the Supreme Government, such as those relating to intervention and the interpretation of treaties, could be referred.

Here, then, we have the outline of a scheme which may be broadly called federation, though it does not closely resemble any existing federal constitution. In reality, it would be another application of the method of Government by Conference which is the way in which we manage the joint affairs of the British Commonwealth of Nations. The machinery of consultation between Ministers representing the various Executive Governments, with the decisions embodied in consequential legislation in the individual States, is now in normal and regular operation. It is definitely recognised and given permanent structure in the organic Memorandum of the Imperial Conference of 1926, which is the new Magna Carta of the self-governing part of the British Empire.

It is conceivable that this method, with suitable modifications, might be applied to that other great British Empire, the Empire of India. It would be novel and experimental: a fresh contribution to political science; but such contributions we are constantly making, and we usually contrive to render them in practice serviceable and efficient. It may be that out of the present unrest and confusion in the Indian political arena some such plan will be evolved to bring symmetry and harmony into the whole complex organism, and to set all the divergent interests working in unison for the general welfare. And if there is any weight in the considerations set forth in the foregoing pages this end cannot be reached without the consent and willing co-operation of the Indian States.

# BIBLIOGRAPHY

Sir Charles Aitchison: *Treaties, Engagements, and Sunnuds relating to India.* (Revised and continued by the Indian Foreign Department.)

Sir C. L. Tupper: *Our Indian Protectorate.* (1893.)

Sir W. Lee-Warner: *The Protected Princes of India.* (1894.)

[The two last-named books contain much valuable information, and Lee-Warner's is written with considerable literary ability. Both, however, give prominence to the views prevalent in official circles at the time they were issued, and should be read with the qualifications suggested in the preceding pages.]

For the States in the past, good histories of India should be consulted, such as Vincent Smith's *Oxford History of India,* Sir William Hunter's *Short History of the Indian Peoples,* and the volumes of the "Rulers of India" Series.

Statistics and other information will be found in the *Imperial Gazetteer of India; The Indian States,* published for the Indian Government; and the *Indian Year Book.*

# INDIA *during the*

# SECOND WORLD WAR

CAPTAIN PETER WRIGHT
COLONEL D. H. COLE
SIR STAFFORD CRIPPS

ARMY BUREAU OF CURRENT AFFAIRS

ISBN: 978-1-910375-47-1